Sacred Jubilee

An Illustrated Devotion for Lent and Easter

Sacred Jubilee is a visual Journey through the historic lectionary of the Christian church. Illustrations by Patti Miller depict the readings of the church year based on the Revised Common Lectionary Series B, and are accompanied by words of devotion written by pastors from across the United States. This work is done to the Glory of God to proclaim the saving message of the Gospel of Jesus Christ.

Contributors:

Rev. Dr. Ralph Blomenberg

Rev. Philip Bloch

Rev. James Rodriguez, Jr

Vicar Coleman Geraci

Illustrations by Patti R. Miller

ISBN-13: 978-0-9994518-3-0

Hymn references are from Lutheran Service Book. St. Louis: Concordia Publishing House. 2006

Ash Wednesday

Joel 2:12-19 2 Corinthians 5:20b, 6:10 Matthew 6:1-6, 16-21

"Dust you are, and to dust you will return." With blackened thumb or finger, fine particles of ash mixed with oil trace a grainy cross on the forehead. Ash Wednesday strikes some as being a morbid occasion, while for others it is a renewing experience. It depends, really, on who is the focus of the day.

The words about returning to the dust focus on us and bring us down to earth. We are creatures, after all, not self-made persons. We have great dreams and goals. We are capable of amazing acts of discovery and invention and service, but given enough time, all of these will come to an end.

But more than creatures, we are *fallen* creatures. The words about returning to the dust were spoken by a Creator deeply offended that a man and woman He made with His own hands chose to defy Him as if He were the enemy of their aspirations. God had breathed His own breath of life into them. Without His breath, there is only death.

We hear enough, and think enough, about death and dying that we don't need another reminder to know what lies before us. And so the ashes, and the cross, lift our eyes and hearts to focus on where the solution to death and sin is.

For thousands of years, ashes have been a sign of sorrow for sin and humility before God. As we receive them, we are identified not as proud individuals plotting our own course despite God, but those who acknowledge our Lord and confess our sins to Him. God exalts those who humble themselves before Him and forgives the repentant.

And the cross-shape of the ashes shows how He did it. It was by humbling Himself in an unimaginable way that He exalts us! The Son of God empties Himself, humbles Himself, to be born with human flesh. He is what we have failed to be: obedient in every way. Yet, He accepts what we are due: death as the result of sin.

But His body, crucified for us, did not turn to dust. It was raised in glory! And all who believe in Him shall live, even though we die, and our dust will be raised in glory when He returns! Dust you are–but for Christ's sake, you are loved, restored, and alive!

Rev. Dr. Ralph Blomenberg

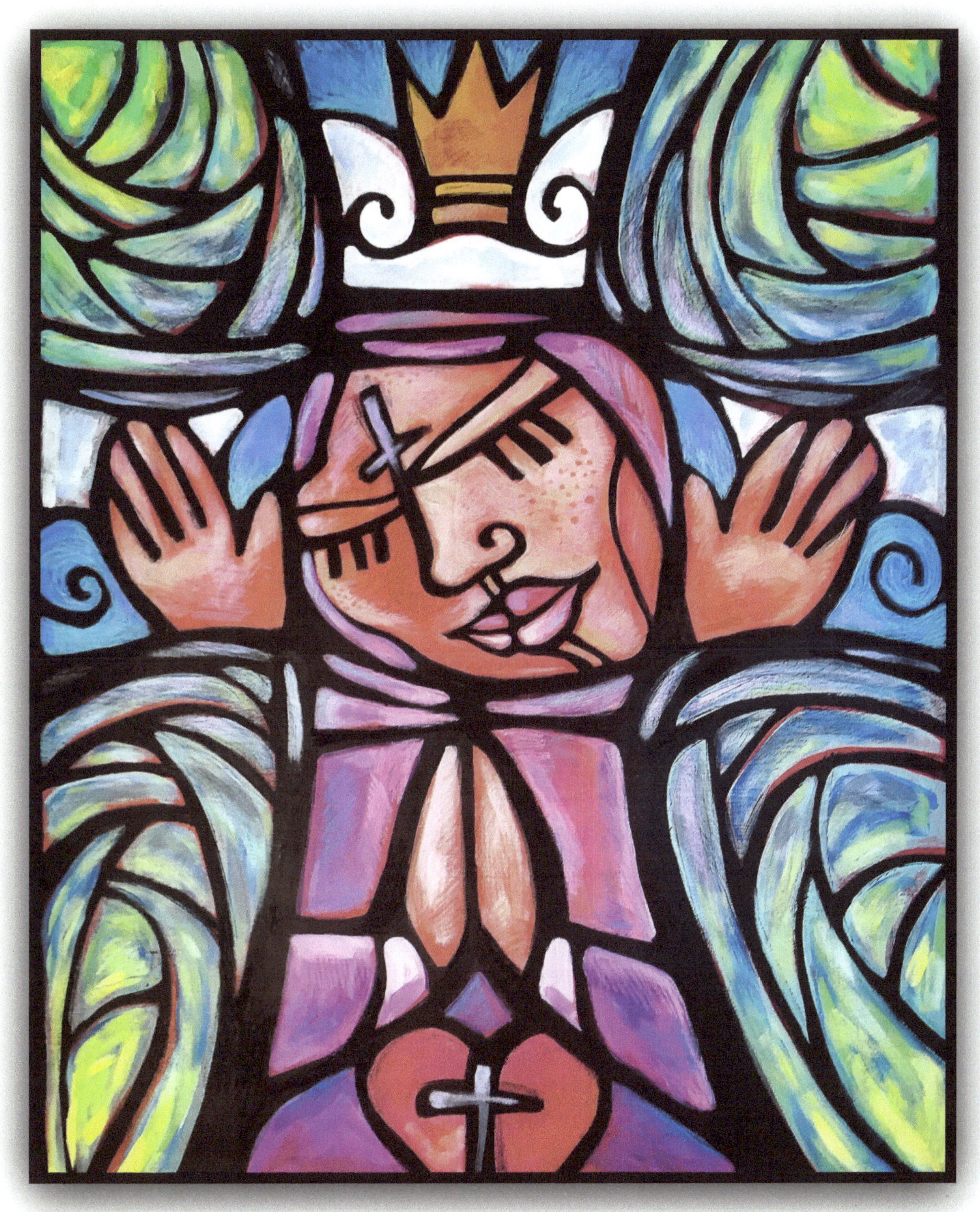

“Raised in Glory” - Acrylic on Wood Panel

First Sunday in Lent

Genesis 22:1-18 James 1:12-18 Mark 1:9-15

So Abraham called the name of that place, "The LORD will provide." Genesis 22:14

To **say** "the Lord will provide" is a statement of faith. To **live** by that expression can be a much harder statement of trust. Abraham and Sarah learned that lesson more than once, and learned it the hard way! Their experience inspires and encourages us, who may want their faith without enduring the way they learned it.

A childless couple late in life, they may have resigned themselves to being without heirs. They found that God does not forget or renege on His promises. Miraculously, Sarah conceived and bore Isaac! The Lord provided the joy of their life, and their hope!

But on Mount Moriah, Abraham's heart and mind must have been racing, and questioning. Was it really God's voice that called him to make a sacrifice of faith of this long-awaited and so beloved son? If so, how would the Lord still provide the promised heir? The Lord provided faith, even under duress, to leave things in God's hands.

What relief Abraham felt when the voice of God intervened, and a ram was provided in place of Isaac as sacrifice! A faith already strong grew even more trusting that day. But Abraham's faith looked well beyond that event to the promise of descendants like the sand of the sea and the stars in the sky.

God provided a partial fulfillment of that promise in you and me. But it was a far more costly provision than what took place on Moriah. God's only, and dearly-beloved Son, walked beneath the burden of a cross to another mountain, Calvary by name. When the time came for His life to be offered, no substitute was provided.

And for good reason. There is no substitute for Jesus. He is the only suitable substitute for you and me. Scripture says He was made a sacrifice for our sins. His innocent blood was shed for us and paid our debt. His life was given so that we would be spared a destiny worse than death.

Whatever our need, God will provide for you and me, too. Paul says, "If God did not spare His own Son, but offered him up for you, how will He not also freely give us all things?" *We pray: O faithful Lord, increase my faith and trust. Amen*

Rev. Dr. Ralph Blomenberg

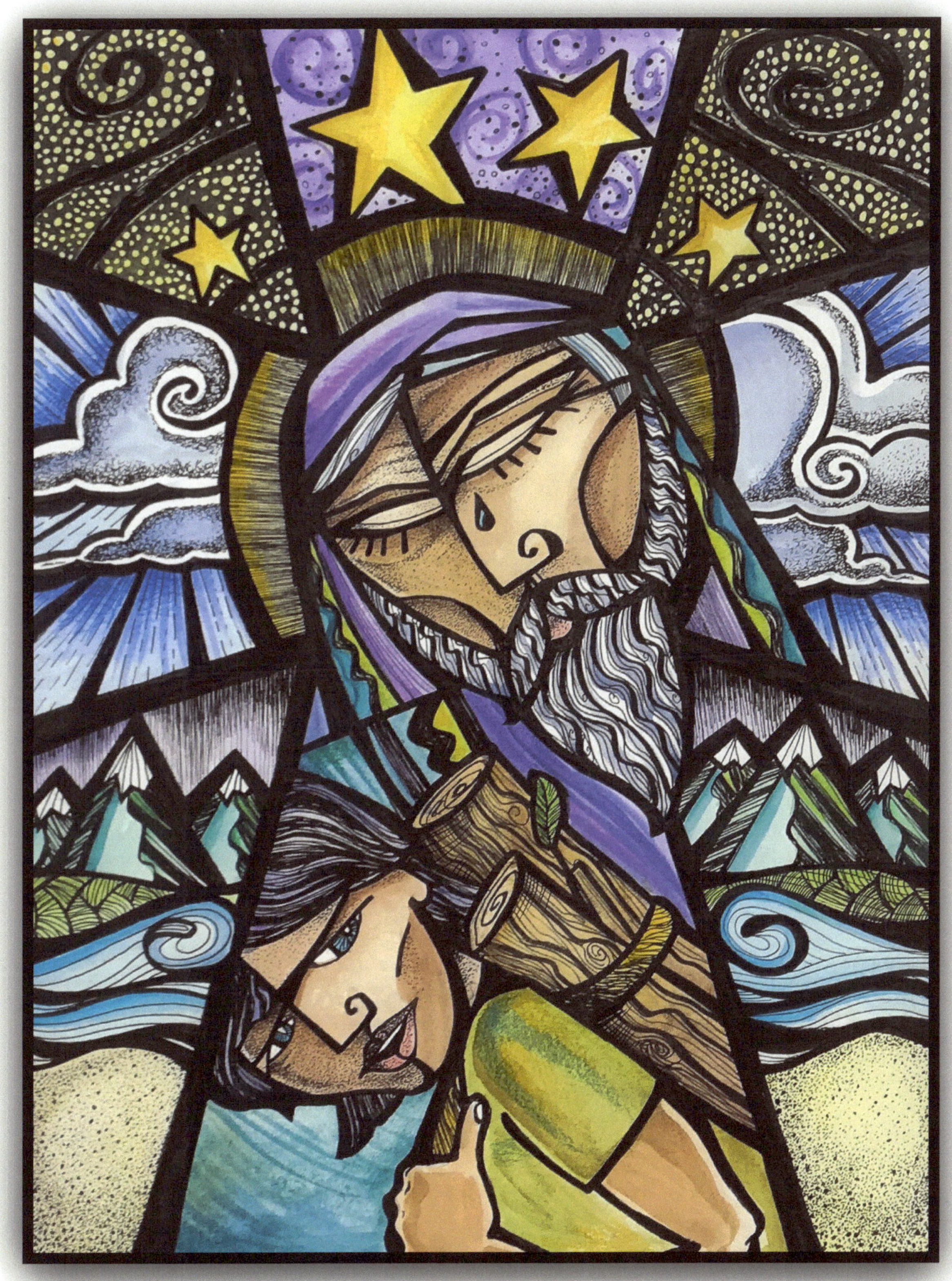

“The Lord Will Provide” - Watercolor, Ink and Pencil

Second Sunday in Lent

Genesis 17:1-7, 15-16 Romans 5:1-11 Mark 8:27-38

...[Jesus] rebuked Peter and said, "Get behind me, Satan! For you are not setting your mind on the things of **God**, *but on the things of man."* Mark 8:33

The foundation of the Christian faith is justification – that is, I am holy before God, not because of anything I've done, but by what Jesus did on the cross, suffering and dying for my sins. And I know that Jesus' work has been accepted by the Father because of Jesus' resurrection. And while I rejoice in that good news, I still live in a world in which I am tempted every day by the devil. And I look to Jesus' example of how to resist the devil – combating Satan's lures with God's Word.

But do I always get it right – fighting back against our enemy the devil? No! But it doesn't mean God loves me less. And it doesn't mean I'm headed to hell. I do need to remember who Jesus is and what He has done. Jesus is God's Son who came into the world to save. And to save He had to die.

Many people like to think of Jesus as the easy-going Jesus, the fun-loving Jesus, never-suffer-and-die kind of Jesus. But that's just what Jesus came to do – suffer and die. And we're called to follow Him, for that is the cost of being His disciple. It's hard for us to swallow, but that is the cross we are to take up.

God loves us. Love led Jesus to the cross. Love stretched out His arms. Love bared His back. Love offered His brow. Love was set in place with nails and poured out upon the earth in blood. Love gave everything to save you, to forgive you, to redeem you. Love died and Love rose on the third day because God is Love and nothing triumphs over God: not sin, not death, not devil, nothing!

The love of God will get us through our times of temptation and trials. For Jesus has overcome the world, overcome the devil, and has overcome death. We find strength and solace in His victory.

Rev. James Rodriguez, Jr

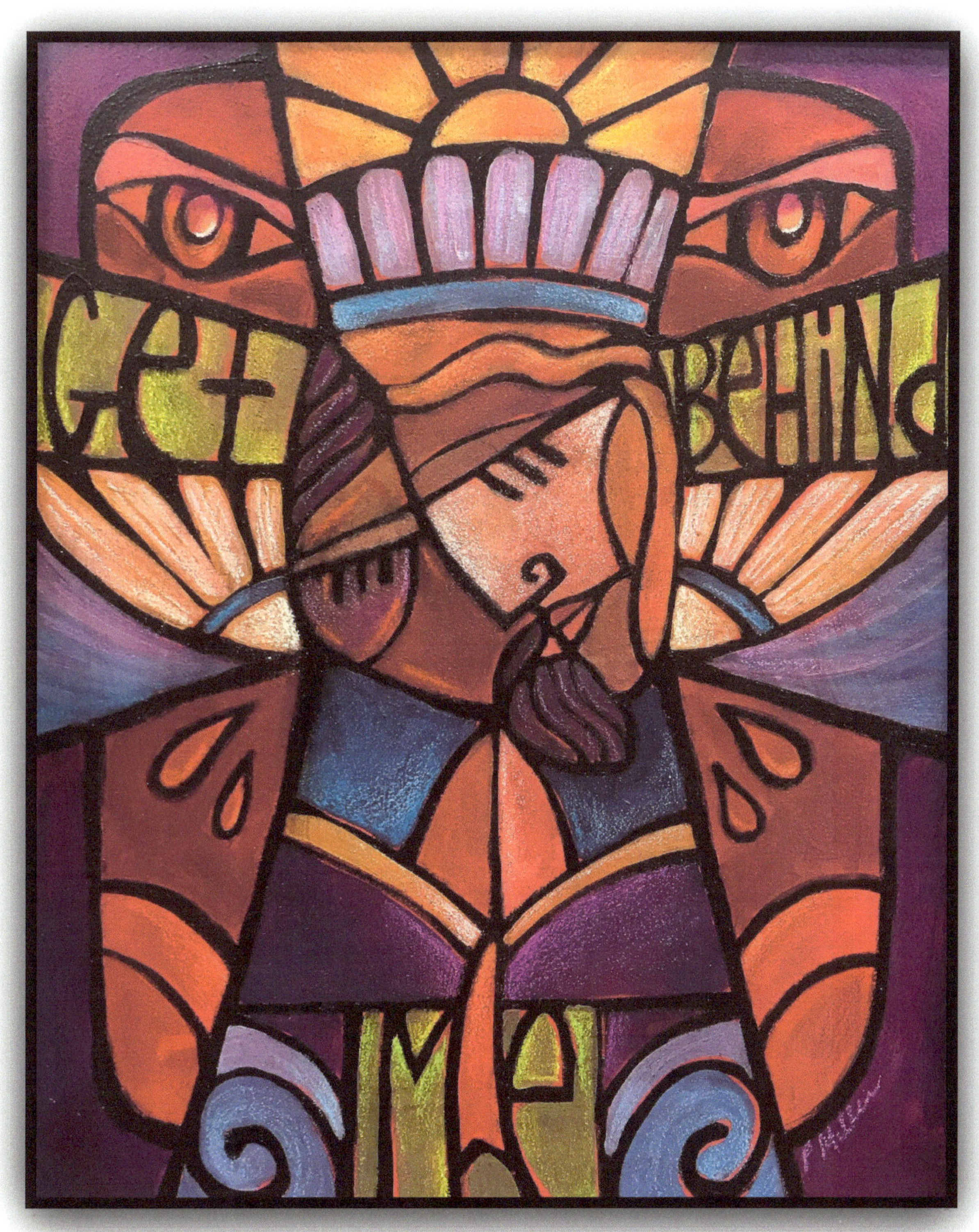

"Get Behind Me" - Acrylic and Oil Pencil on Wood Panel

Third Sunday in Lent

Exodus 20:1-17 1 Corinthians 1:18-31 John 2:13-25

The Crucified Christ is an affront to the natural man – that is why Paul describes it as foolishness and a stumbling block. Natural man tries to find some way around a bleeding, suffering, dying Jesus as what reconciles us to God. Natural man tries to substitute anything he can in the place of a Crucified Christ. He will seek a Christ that is a nice example for him to aspire to; a Christ who helps him overcome some faults in personality and attitude; a Christ who embodies a certain political or social agenda. Natural man will seek a Christ that fits hits own conceptions of how God works. But none of these alternative Christs solve the problem at the heart of natural man: None atone for sin.

The only way sin can be atoned for is the blood of a sacrifice. The only way sinful nature can be overcome is by a Sinless One taking it upon Himself. The only way the consequence of sin can be overcome is by that Sinless One overcoming them – by overcoming death. The only One who does this is the Crucified One. His sacrifice atones for our sin; He takes sin upon Himself and gives out His Righteousness; His resurrection conquers death. The good news is that this Crucified One extends that victory to you.

As the church, when you are asked what the church proclaims - the answer is simple: Jesus of Nazareth, the Crucified One. You proclaim that this Crucified One has risen from the dead; that forgiveness of sins comes in His name; that reconciliation to God comes through His blood. The church is the mouth house of God where the word of the Cross – the message of the Crucified One – goes forth. And there is no other message more important for the world.

We preach Christ crucified because the Crucified One is the wisdom and power of God. We don't talk this way because we enjoy gory things. We talk this way because there is no other Christ than the One with nails driven into his hands and feet; the One with a spear driven into his side. There is no other Christ than the One who was mocked and beaten, who bled and died on Calvary. The Christ, the Savior of the world, is the Crucified One. And there is no other name by which man can be saved.

Vicar Coleman Geraci

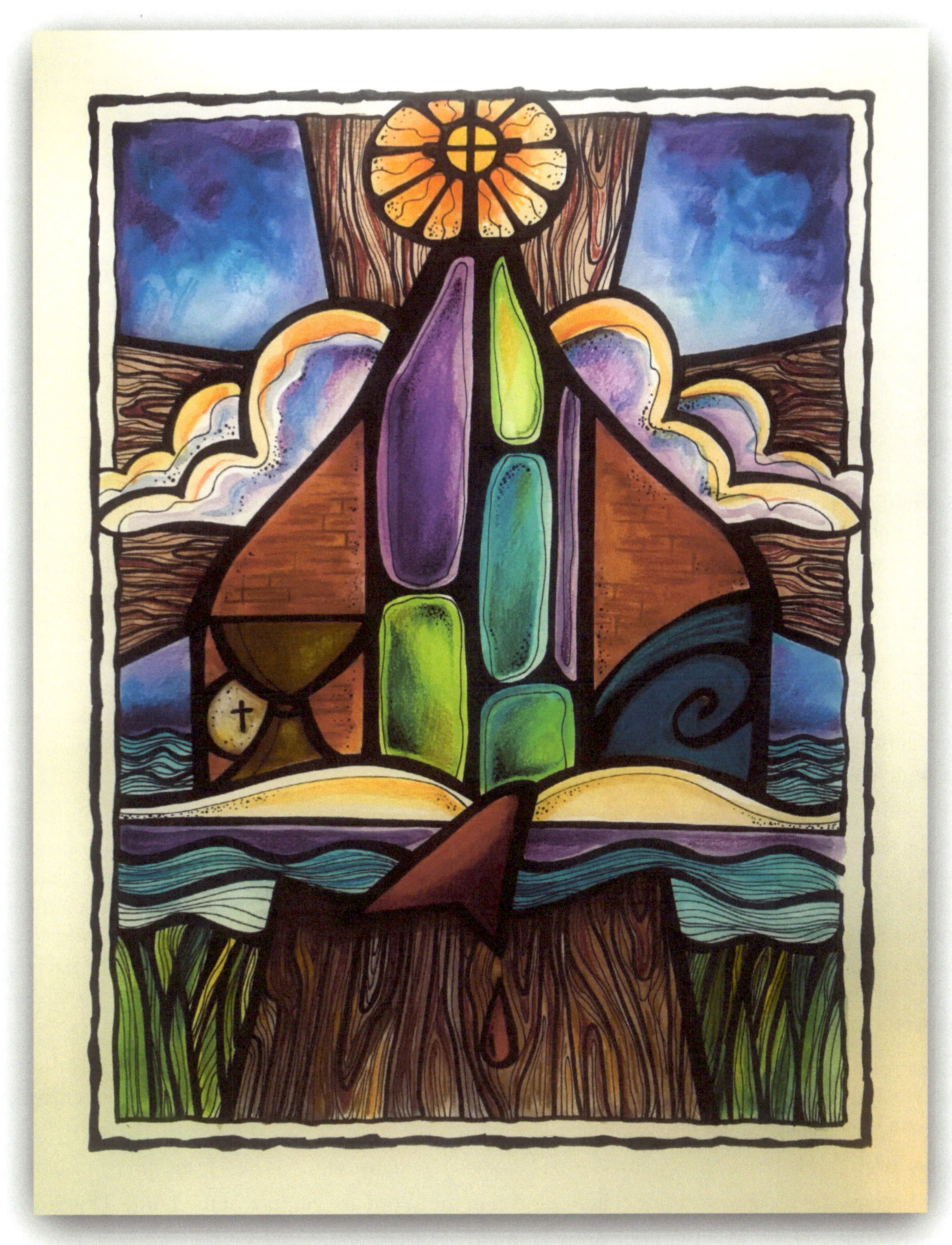

“Talk This Way” - Ink and Watercolor

Fourth Sunday in Lent

Numbers 21:4-9   Ephesians 2:1-10   John 3:14-21

And as Moses lifted up the serpent in the wilderness, so must the Son of Man be lifted up, that whoever believes in him may have eternal life. John 3:14-15

"Look a snake!" Did your skin crawl or did you peek down at the floor when you read that line? Many people are frightened of these slithering reptiles. Even viewing them behind thick glass at the local zoo makes them shudder! Those who handle snakes and work with them tell us there is no need to be frightened of these creatures. They say that snakes are more afraid of humans than we are of them!

But don't tell that to the Israelites in Numbers chapter 21! The fiery, or poisonous, snakes were on the loose and were in attack mode! Here was not the situation where 'if you just leave the deadly snakes alone; they will leave you alone.' No, they were biting the people of Israel under the leadership of Moses in the wilderness wanderings! The serpents were after them, and people were dying! If something was not done and done quickly, there would be no one left alive!

God's accusing Law, like these snakes, will not leave sinners who violate His Holy Law alone! It's not a case where if we ignore God's Law, we have nothing to fear from it! The Law of God, like those fiery serpents, is on the attack! The Law is after us, and it knows where to find us! And there is venom, deadly venom, in its bite! One bite–just one nibble of the Law against the sinner brings certain death!

In the desert, God in mercy instructed Moses to make a bronze serpent and place it on a pole, and then, when anyone looked to that serpent trusting in God's Word, they would live. Centuries later, Jesus Christ was raised on a Roman cross that all who fix their eyes on Him as their Savior from sin in faith will live even amid a dying world. Jesus says in John 3:15-16, "just as Moses lifted up the serpent in the wilderness, so must the Son of Man be lifted up, that whoever believes in Him may have eternal life. "For God so loved the world, that He gave His only Son, that whoever believes in Him should not perish but have eternal life."

When God's Law bites you and accuses you--and it always will, for we are sinners who daily disobey it--but when the Law does sink its fangs into your conscience, Jesus is here for you so that you may fix your eyes on Him and be healed and forgiven.

Jesus forgives, He heals, He comforts! And His shed blood gives life to you! Jesus' precious blood is the anti-venom, and it is always, *always* here for you in the Word and Supper of the Lord! Don't turn away from but turn to Jesus in faith! Look upon Him and be saved!

Rev. Philip Bloch

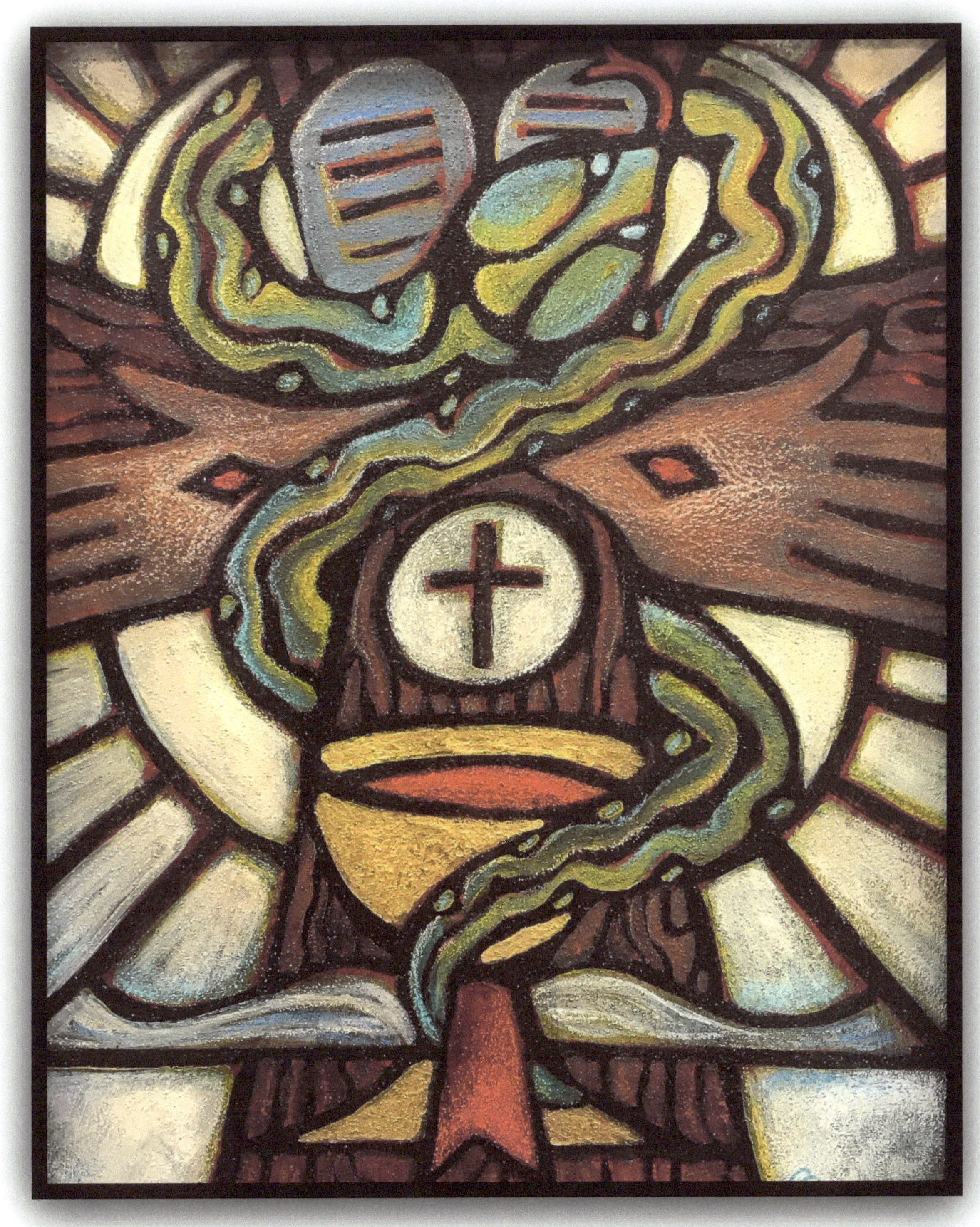

"A Biting Message" - Acrylic and Oil Pencil on Wood Panel

Fifth Sunday in Lent

Jeremiah 31:31-34   Hebrews 5:1-10   Mark 10:32-45

And they were on the road, going up to Jerusalem, and Jesus was walking ahead of them. And they were amazed, and those who followed were afraid. Mark 10:32

The unexpected things people do may cause us to wonder if they are crazy or heroic. The jury was still out on Jesus as the disciples follow after Him to Jerusalem. Some were likely wondering if they might want to follow from a safer distance!

It was not that Jerusalem was by nature a dangerous place. It was the holiest of places for the Jews, since it was the location of their Temple. This time of the year, it was probably safer, bristling with soldiers protecting against possible riots around Passover.

Thousands of pilgrims would descend upon Jerusalem to worship for the Passover. But it was dangerous for Jesus. There was a price on his head. Not because He had done any crime, but because He was perceived as a threat to the leaders of the Jewish faith.

He was too popular. He healed the sick and cast out demons and raised the dead. He called them out on practices and teachings that were not based on Scripture. He exposed their hypocrisy. They would not stand for it. He had to go.

Knowing what they intended to do, Jesus could have stayed away and prolonged His life. But with perfect sanity, Jesus set his face toward Jerusalem. The good shepherd will lead from the front. His disciples timidly, fearfully, follow Him.

There are times following Jesus for us may be like it was back then. Those who follow Jesus march to a drum the world thinks is foolish. After all, in this day and age, who forgives those who hurt you, instead of getting even? Jesus, and those who follow him.

Who is more concerned about storing up treasures in heaven than hoarding things here? Jesus, and those who follow him. Who dares confront sinners in love to help them find a better way? Jesus, and those who follow him.

What a privilege that Jesus has called us to follow Him! He has already secured the victory, the journey to eternity. Jesus has defeated sin, death, and the devil, and all who are in him shall reign with him. We pray: Lord Jesus, give me faith today to follow You, no matter what. Amen

Rev. Dr. Ralph Blomenberg

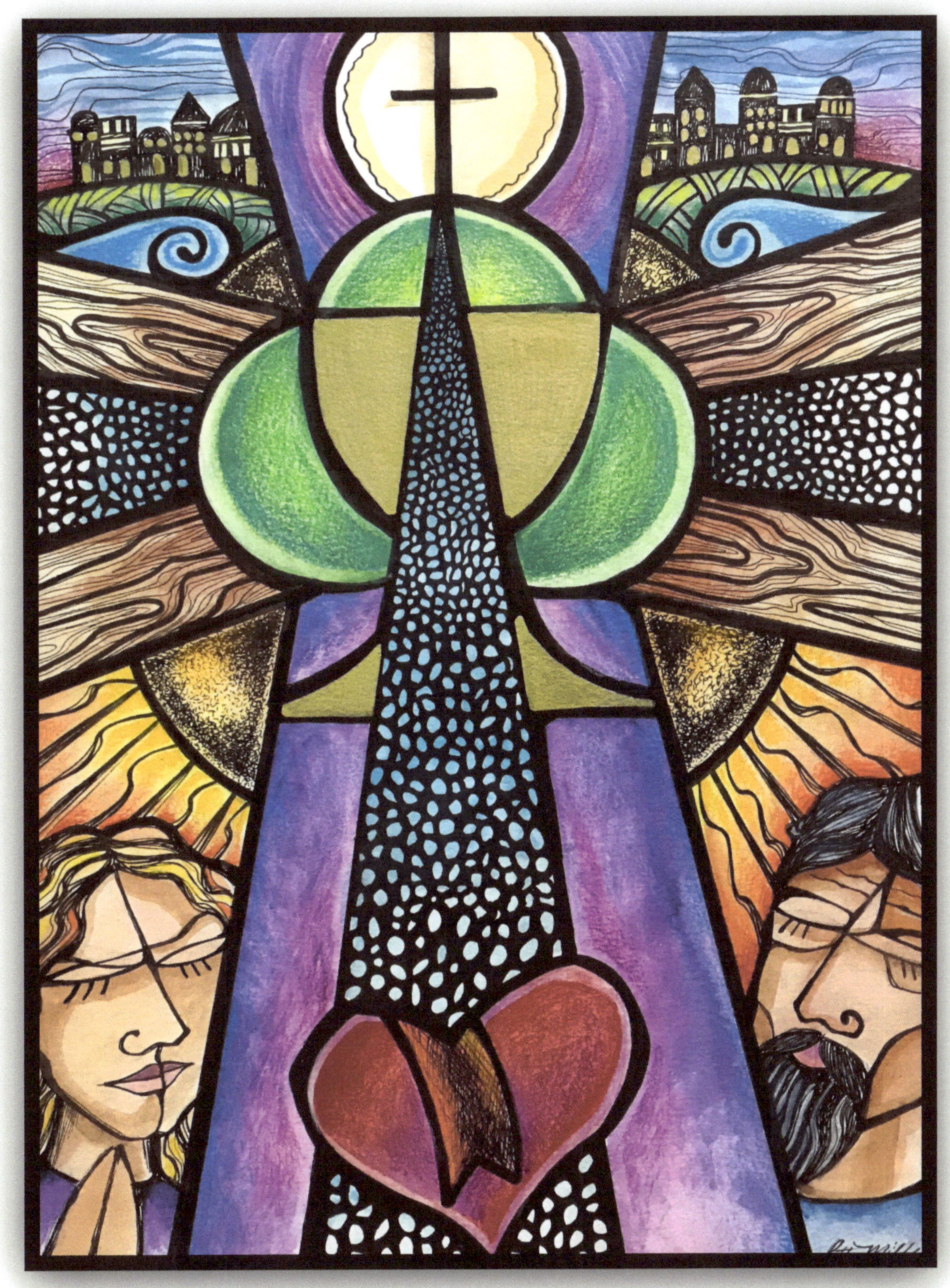

"Marching to Madness" - Ink and Watercolor

SUNDAY OF THE PASSION

Zechariah 9:9-12   Philippians 2:5-11   John 12:20-43

"Hosanna! Blessed is he who comes in the name of the Lord, even the King of Israel!" John 12:13

The text above finds its context in the arrival of Jesus into Jerusalem on that day we call Palm Sunday. He came into the city riding a donkey to the adoration of many people. He came into the city with the hopes of many that He was the "Messiah," the Savior who would come with power.

Oh, He had shown His power on many occasions – making the lame walk, making the blind see, making the deaf hear, casting out demons, even raising people from the dead on three different occasions. But as this week moved on people began to have second thoughts about Jesus because He wasn't using His power. And in our society, not using power means you don't have power. Not using power means that you embrace weakness. And nobody likes weakness. Weakness suffers and weakness dies.

Jesus doesn't do as we want nor as we would expect. And this is the gospel of our Lord. For His weakness is our strength. His humiliation is our glory. His death is our life. And His resurrection the certainty of our eternity.

When Jesus is lifted up, when He is crucified, when He is at His weakest, He is taking down our enemies and drawing men to Himself. He covers our sins, He debilitates the devil, and He destroys death. Jesus loves you to death – His death. Jesus loved you with a divine, eternal, saving-from-hell kind of love. And though this love appears weak, it is anything but weak.

Love that dies for us is stronger than death. Jesus appears on this cross to be weak and lowly and humiliated. Yet here on this cross Jesus is strongest, loving you in a way that is both gentle and powerful.

Rev. James Rodriguez, Jr

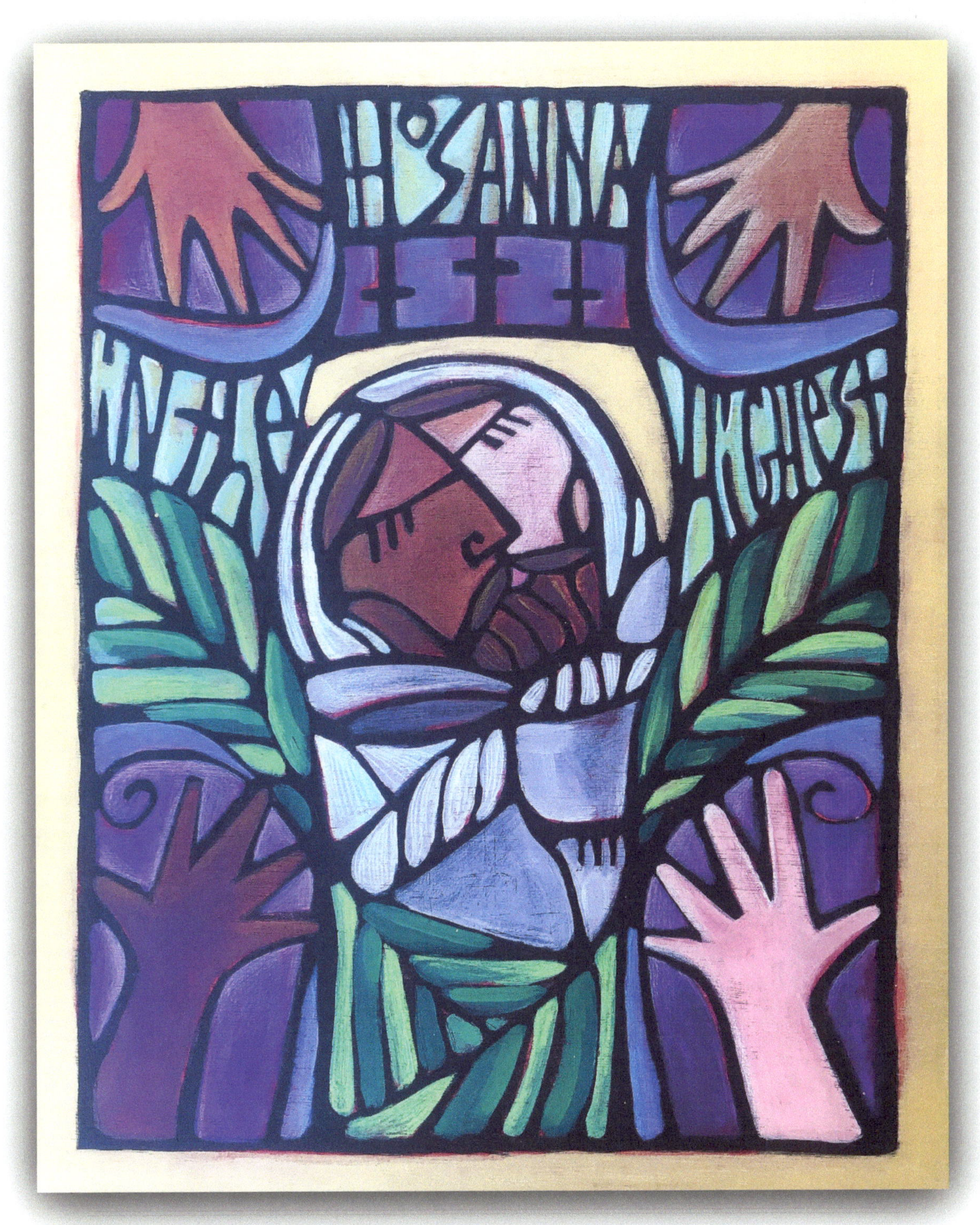

"Hosanna" - Acrylic and Oil Pencil on Wood Panel

Maundy Thursday

Exodus 24:3-11 1 Corinthians 10:16-17 Mark 14:12-26

And as they were eating, he took bread, and after blessing it broke it and gave it to them, and said, "Take; this is my body." And he took a cup, and when he had given thanks he gave it to them, and they all drank of it. And he said to them, "This is my blood of the[a] covenant, which is poured out for many. Mark 14:22-24

Maundy comes from the Latin word *mandatum*, which means "commandment." Jesus gave many commands to His disciples that night in the Upper Room, including "love one another" (John 13:34) and "wash one another's feet" (John 13:14). Perhaps most wonderful of all, are those "commands" that Jesus gave when He instituted His Holy Supper: "Take," "eat," and "drink" (Matt. 26:26-28, ESV). The invitation to the Lord's Supper is both commandment and promise, for, with these words, Jesus gives us His true Body and Blood for the forgiveness of sins.

In the Lord's Supper, there is more than a merely spiritual presence. There is an actual, physical, real, sacramental presence of Jesus' Body and Blood "in, with, and under" the common earthly elements of bread and wine. We do not know how this miracle takes place. By faith, we believe that it does because of the simple words of Jesus: "This is my body" and "This is my blood of the covenant, which is poured out for many" (Mark 14:22, 24).

On Maundy Thursday Jesus gave us His Supper as a meal of remembrance and forgiveness for the entire Christian community–"poured out for many" (Mark 14:22). The Lord's Supper is one of the means of grace by which Jesus is truly present with His Church. The Lord's Supper shows forth our unity of faith–and it also makes us one. As Norman Nagel once put it so well, "The sacramental body 'bodies' together the ecclesiastical 'body.'" In the Lord's Supper, Jesus gives us one bread, one cup, and one body to make all Christians one! Christ invites us to "take and eat, take and drink, for the forgiveness of sins" (Matt. 26:26-28). And in this way, we participate in His Body and Blood.

"The cup of blessing that we bless, is it not a participation in the blood of Christ? The bread that we break, is it not a participation in the body of Christ? Because there is one bread, we who are many are one body, for we all partake of the one bread" (1 Cor. 10:16-17). And by the body and blood of Christ, you are forgiven of all your sins!

Rev. Philip Bloch

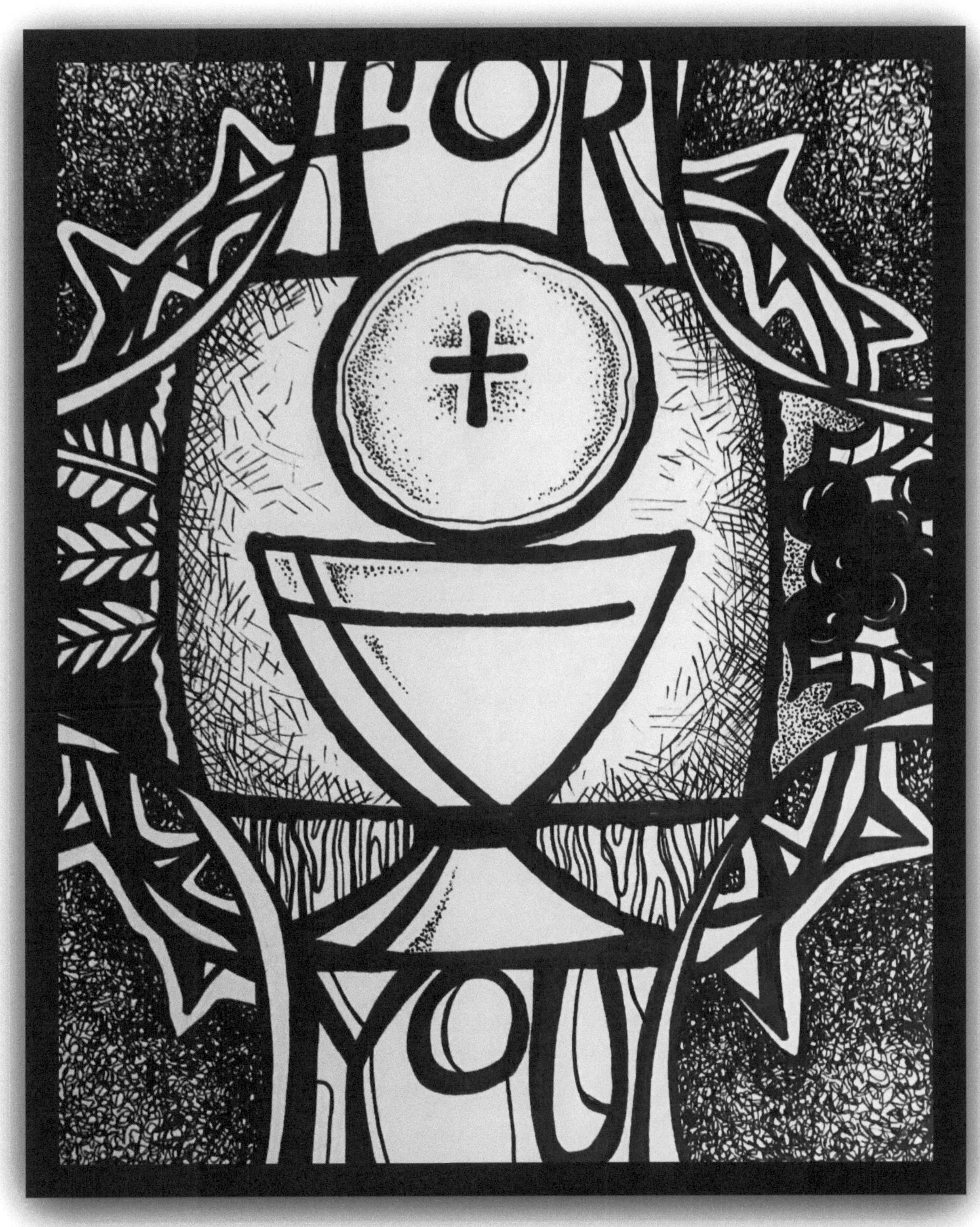

"The Blood of The Covenant" - Pen and Ink

Good Friday

Isaiah 52:13-53:8 Hebrews 4:14-16; 5;7-9 John 19:17-30

When Jesus had received the sour wine, He said, "It is finished," and He bowed His head and gave up His spirit. - John 19:30

It's a simple and cliche statement: Words mean things. Words have an impact. Regardless of whether that impact is joyful or painful, words can change the course of life. So it is with the words of our Lord, "It is finished."

As Jesus dies on the cross, commending Himself into God the Father's hands, He declares those words to the whole world. But what is finished? What does this mean?

Jesus has finished His work. In the Gospel according to St. John, Jesus has been on a mission from God since the opening verses. He is the Word made flesh, the Lamb of God who takes away the sin of the world. He is the One who demonstrated who He is by what He has done. He turned water into wine, healed the sick, fed 5,000 people, raised the dead. And now, He glorifies God by willingly going to the cross.

On that cross, Jesus places Himself as the substitute to take on the punishment that we deserve. We deserve the death Jesus died – the hell He endured on the Cross. We deserve to be the ones rejected, despised, and forsaken by God.

But God is merciful. God reveals His true nature to us as Jesus tells us in John 3:16-17, "For God so loved the world that He gave His only Son, that whoever believes in Him should not perish but have eternal life. For God did not send His Son into the world to condemn the world, but to save it through Him."

The words, "It is finished," declare Jesus has completed all of which He set forth to do: to win the forgiveness of sins; to conquer death, hell, and the devil. And He does this all for you. When He went willingly to the Cross, He went there with you in mind. He went there to be the One to reconcile you with God the Father. And He did it.

Jesus words are final. His Words are true. His Words endure forever. His Words change you. "It is finished."

Amen.
Vicar Coleman Geraci

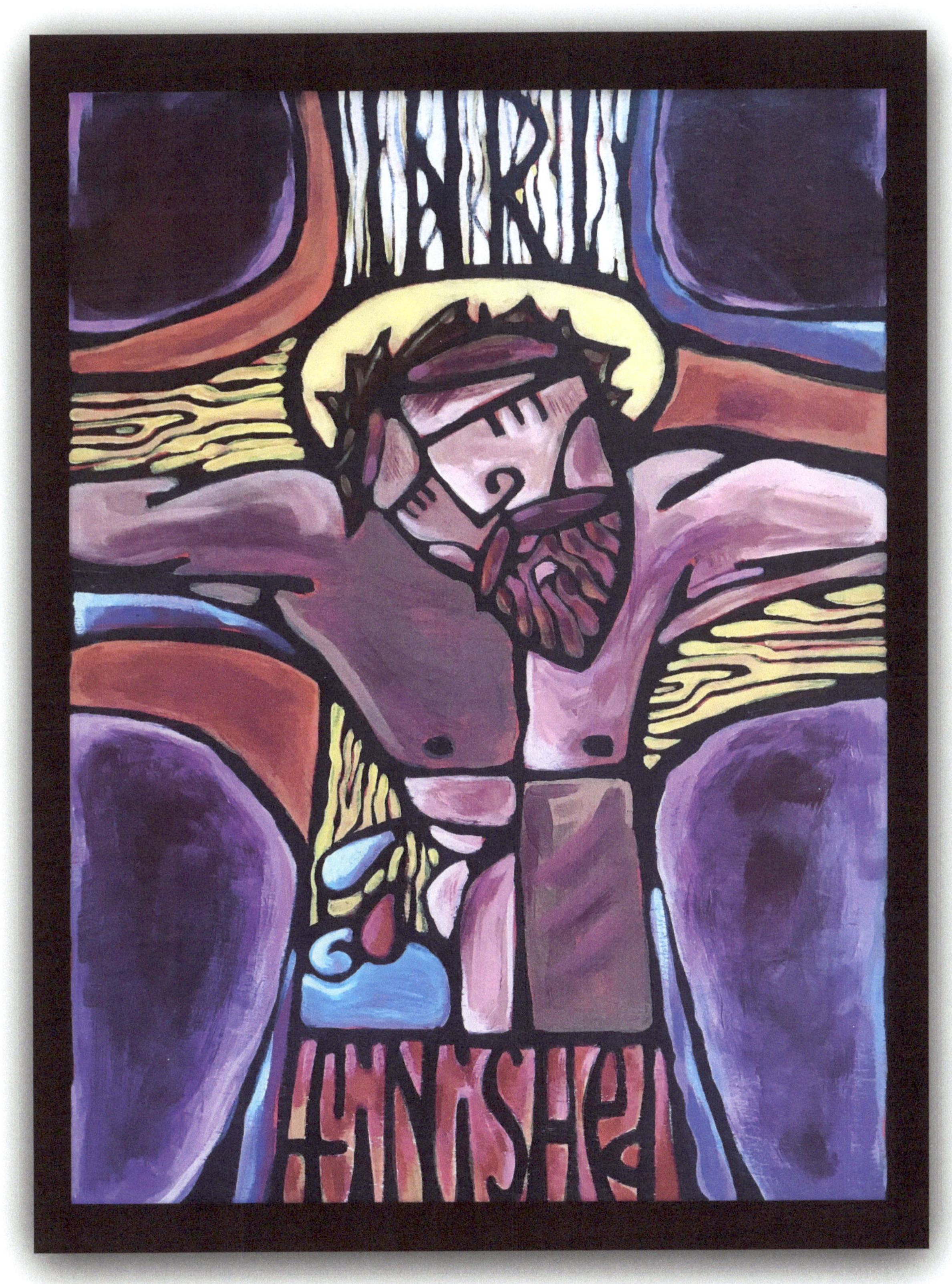

"It Is Finished" - Acrylic and Oil Pencil on Wood Panel

Easter

Isaiah 25:6-9   1 Corinthians 15:1-11   Mark 16:1-8

"Do not be alarmed. You seek Jesus of Nazareth, who was crucified. He has risen; He is not here. See the place where they laid Him." Mark 16:6

We live in an age of virtual reality. People can put on VR Goggles and be immersed in a scene that looks so real it can leave them gasping for breath. But it is just an image. The resurrection of Jesus was not computer generated virtual reality. In a way, virtual reality is the problem Jesus came to solve.

Virtual reality looks real, but is not real. Its first creator was not some computer geek, but a fallen angel. It was Satan who tricked humans to envision the improved reality he said would come from going against God. He lied to them.

And his temptations have made fools of us, too. *Take this, and you will be happy. Do that, and you will be loved. Try this, and you will succeed.* It sounds so inviting. Then the reality hits. Rejection; guilt; addiction; despair.

Easter invites us to move from virtual reality to the truth. Jesus's tomb was empty on Easter. If His enemies had stolen the body, they would have been the first to display it as proof He was dead. If the disciples had stolen it, they would not have died to defend a lie. Jesus talked with them, ate with them, touched them. It is proof that convinces even the most skeptical of them! He is alive!

Easter is not a nice spiritual story to make you feel better. It is proof that God has made you better, through Jesus. It means that the God who raised Jesus from the dead cares an awful lot about foolish sinners like us. He died and rose to forgive you.

Those who see Christianity as a system of rules from a God who wants to restrict our freedom have it backwards. Faith in Jesus frees us to live with the confidence that with God, all things are possible. There is always hope! Even death is not the end.

Jesus comes to us still in real ways: in Words spoken and heard; in bread and wine we can taste. Christ is Risen! He is risen indeed. Alleluia! *We pray: Lord Jesus, help me to live with hope, knowing You live for me today. Amen*

Rev. Dr. Ralph Blomenberg

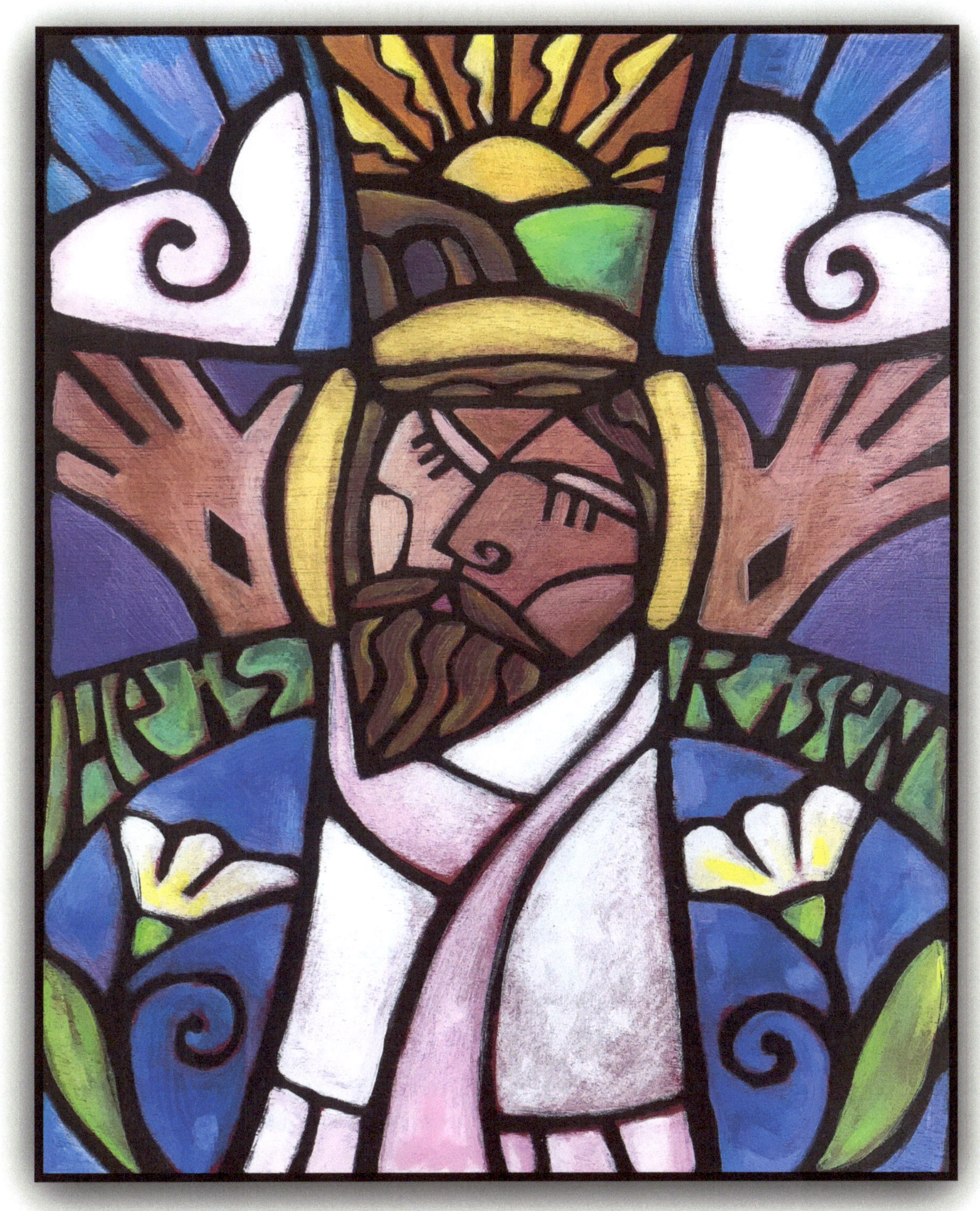

"He is Risen" - Acrylic and Oil Pencil on Wood Panel

SECOND SUNDAY OF EASTER

Acts 4:32-35 1 John 1:1-2:2 John 20:19-31

On the evening of that day, the first day of the week, the doors being locked where the disciples were for fear of the Jews, Jesus came and stood among them and said to them, "Peace be with you." When he had said this, he showed them his hands and his side. Then the disciples were glad when they saw the Lord. John 20:19-20

From a hardened, dead looking chrysalis emerges the breathtaking beauty of the butterfly! New life springs from what was once considered dead. The butterfly in its transformation is a vivid reminder of our Lord Jesus' resurrection on Easter morning.

Jesus' lifeless body was taken down from the accursed tree on Calvary's hill and wrapped in linen burial clothes and placed into Joseph of Arimathea's newly hewn tomb. A seal was placed, and a detachment of Roman soldiers posted at the command of the Roman procurator Pontius Pilate.

But seal, stone, and soldiers could not prevent our Lord's resurrection! Early on the first day of the week, Christ rose victoriously and appeared to His frightened disciples showing Himself alive and greeting them with "Peace." When Jesus breathed out the Holy Spirit on them, the disciples showed signs of life! Peeking out of the chrysalis of their locked meeting room the disciples′ butterfly wings began to flutter! "We have seen the Lord!" they told the absent Thomas! They were out of their hard shell sounding like disciples of Jesus, and not a dead Jesus, but a risen Jesus!

Eight days later the disciples' butterfly wings looked pretty limp, and back they slunk into their old, hardened shell of fear and unbelief. Once again, they cower in fear behind locked doors! So what does the risen Lord do? Again Jesus comes to them, and He blesses them with His Holy Spirit. Jesus gives them the word of peace, and by the power of the Holy Spirit turns doubting Thomas into confessing Thomas! In confident faith, Thomas exclaims, "My Lord and my God!"

When Jesus left the hard chrysalis of His tomb, He left your sins buried there! Christ buried forever your guilt and condemnation there. So why do we want to crawl back in there? That's not the risen life! Jesus has freed us from the old chrysalis! We are butterflies now! We are free of our sins! God forgives us in Christ! There is no need to live in fear--fear of God, fear of death, fear of judgment, fear of condemnation, fear of others! We are butterflies freed from the old hardened shell of our sins, made beautiful in the waters of our baptisms!

In Holy Baptism, we have died to our old sinful self and have risen to a new life in Christ! We are butterflies! We are free to unfold our wings and fly now, living the risen and ascended life in Christ! We can carry to all the doubting Thomas' out there the glorious message of Easter! Alleluia! Christ is Risen! He is Risen Indeed! Alleluia!

Rev. Philip Bloch

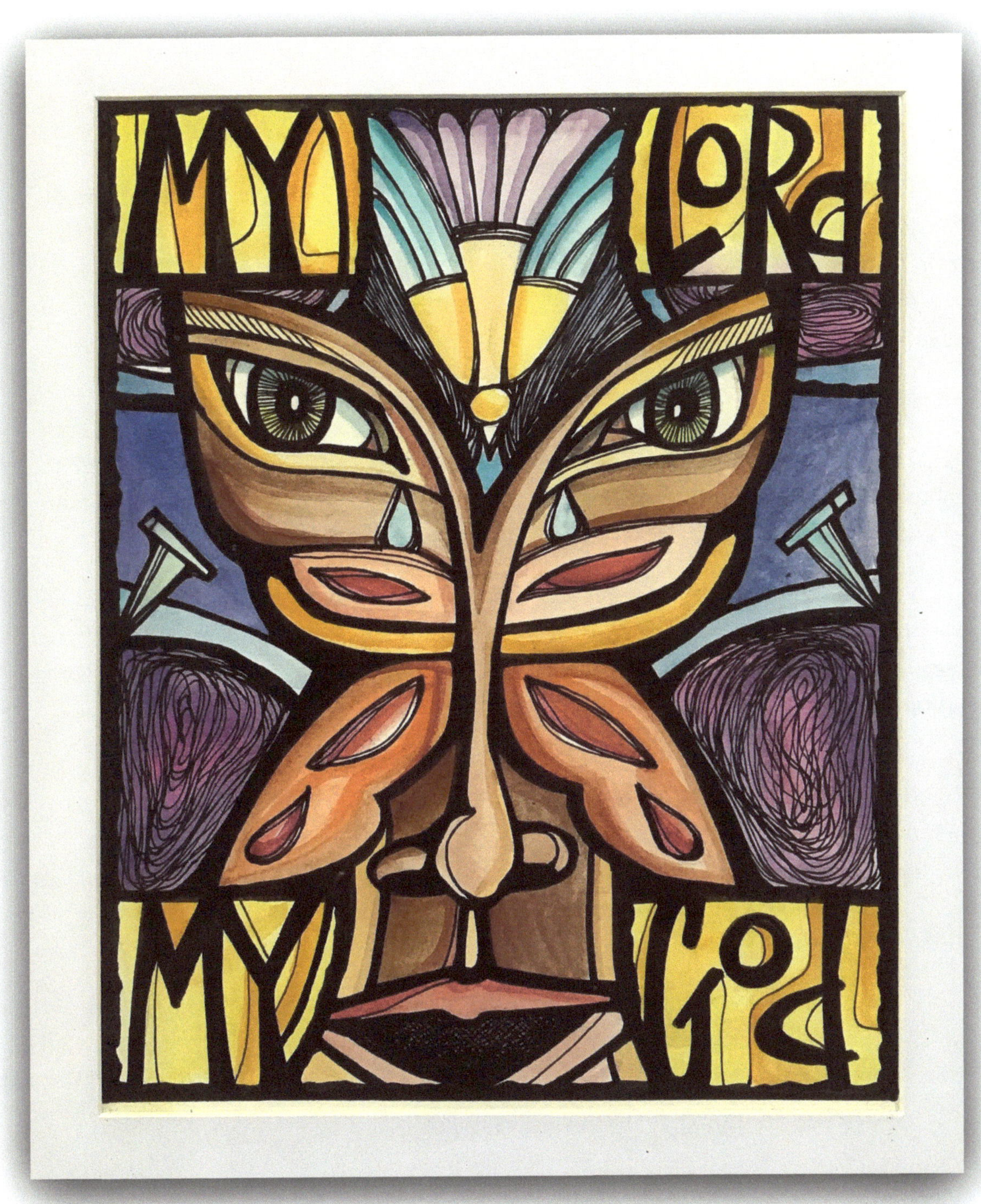

"Fly! Don't Crawl" - Ink and Watercolor

Third Sunday of Easter

Acts 3:11-21, 1 John 3:1-7, Luke 24:36-49

[Jesus] said to them, "This is what I told you while I was still with you: Everything must be fulfilled that is written about me in the Law of Moses, the Prophets and the Psalms." [45] *Then he opened their minds so they could understand the Scriptures.* [46] *He told them, "This is what is written: The Messiah will suffer and rise from the dead on the third day,* [47] *and repentance for the forgiveness of sins will be preached in his name to all nations, beginning at Jerusalem.* Luke 24:44-47

The Bible is a difficult book to understand, even for a mature Christian. Some people see the Bible as just another book to be read, pondered, and then move on to the next book. But for Christians the Bible is God's way of speaking to us today.

The main message about Jesus in the Bible is that He was sent by God to pay for the sins of the world because sin cannot come before a holy, perfect God. So Jesus came into the world, suffered, died, and rose so sins could be forgiven. Jesus executed His Father's plan and now His victory over sin, death, and devil is our victory! Now, that Good News should be shared with the world, which is what this artwork seeks to do.

Studying the Bible is a life-long exercise. And it's one that is never finished. But Christians believe that through regular study of God's Word the Bible becomes more understandable and we are able to more thoroughly inject it into our daily life of faith. Not only does the Bible give us good guidance to live a godly life, it more importantly reminds us every day that we are saved and stand before God as pure and holy because of Jesus' work on the cross and out of the tomb.

The Bible has the power to convert unbelief to belief. It sounds odd to those who don't believe in God, but God has the power to do things that man cannot. As a pastor, I can simply share what God has done in my life, plant that seed in yours, and see what God does with it. But if the journey takes one to belief, then it's going to take that person to the Bible. Enjoy the trip!

Rev. James Rodriguez, Jr

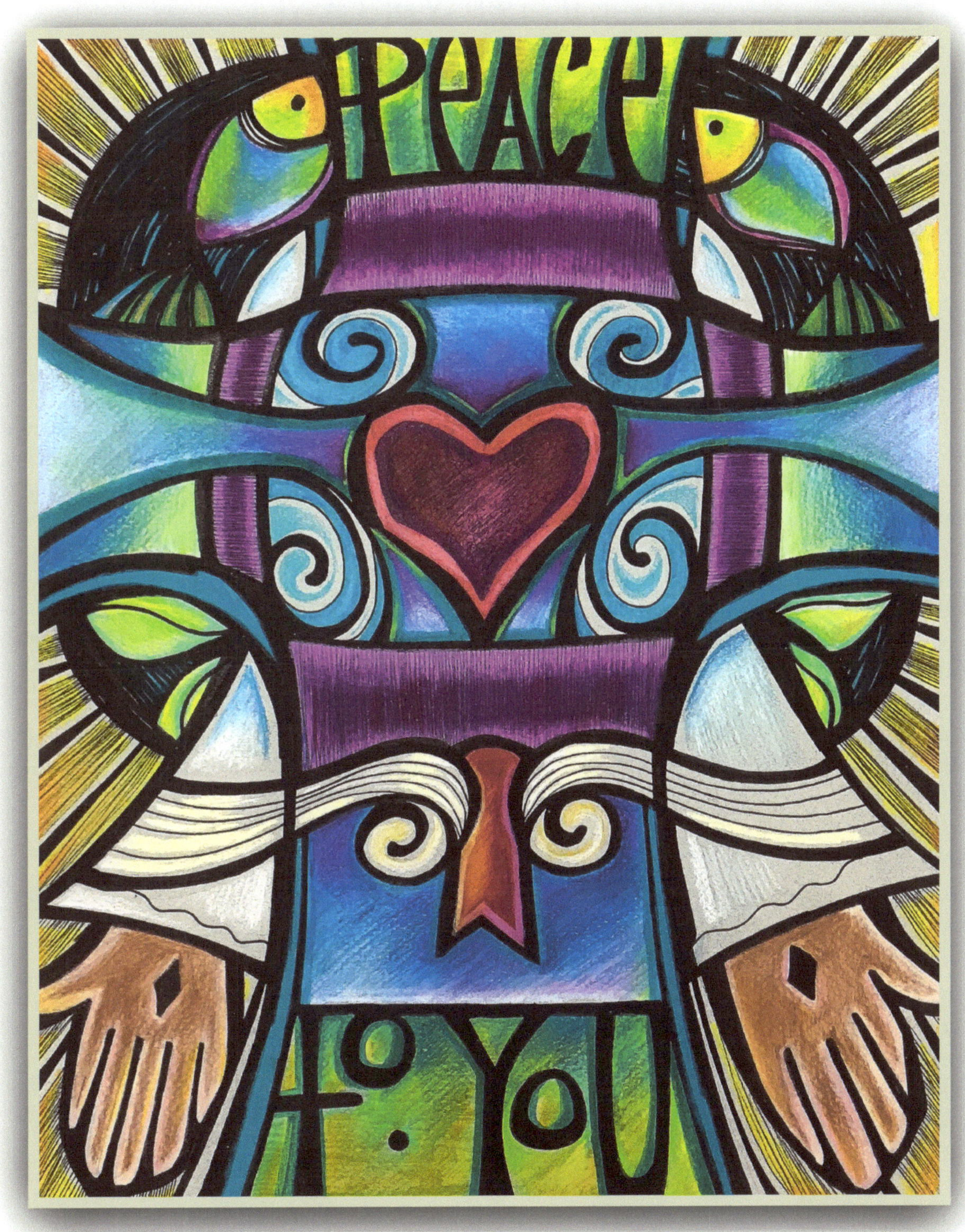

"Understand the Scriptures" - Ink and Watercolor

Fourth Sunday of Easter

Acts 4:1-12 1 John 3:16-24 John 10:11-18

Jesus said, "I am the Good Shepherd. I know My own and My own know Me, just as the Father knows Me and I know the Father; and I lay down My life for the sheep." (John 10:14-15)

Shepherds have a significant place in Scripture. Many of the heroes of the Old Testament were shepherds, Moses and David being two most notable. In the New Testament, shepherds were the first to witness the birth of Christ. St. Paul includes "shepherds" in his list of the people God gives to the church to equip the saints for their life of faith (Ephesians 4). St. Peter commands that those who oversee the church to be shepherds of the flock of God (1 Peter 5). However, only One Person in Scripture declares that He is the Good Shepherd - Jesus of Nazareth. So what sets Jesus apart as the Good Shepherd?

Jesus is the Good Shepherd because of what He does. He is not like the evil shepherds of old that do not care for their flocks, who run and hide at any sign of danger, who let the wolves come and snatch away the sheep. He is not like a hired hand who is only in it for his own benefits. No, Jesus is the One who is willing to protect His sheep at all costs.

Jesus willingly gives His life up for His sheep. He gives it up out of His own authority and He does this to please His Father. Jesus goes through death and hell on the cross for His sheep. He lays down His life for them, so that He may take it up again. And He does just that – He keeps His word. He rises from the dead for His Sheep to be their eternal Good Shepherd.

Jesus is the Good Shepherd who gave His life and rose from the dead to make you a member of His Good Sheep Herd. And as His Good Sheep, He forgives you your sins and leads you into His pastures. He continues to guard and provide for you.

The King of Love my Shepherd is,
Whose goodness faileth never;
I nothing lack if I am His
And He is mine forever.

And so, through all the length of days,
Thy Goodness faileth never.
Good Shepherd, may we sing thy praise,
Within thy house forever.
LSB 709 vs. 1,6
Amen.
Vicar Coleman Geraci

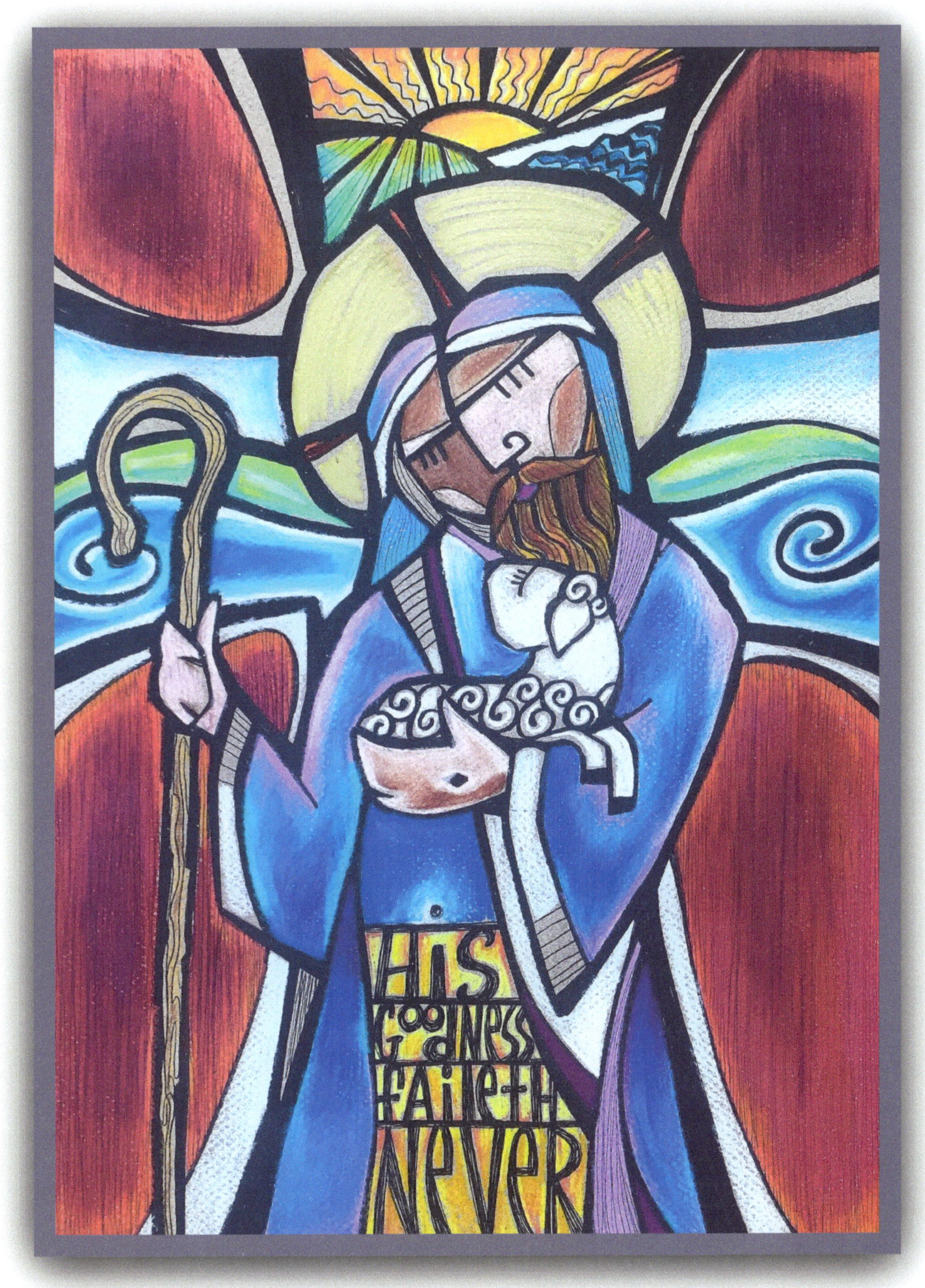

"The Good Sheep Herd?" - Ink and Watercolor

Fifth Sunday of Easter

Acts 8:26-40, 1 John 4:1-11, John 15:1-8

I am the vine; you are the branches. Whoever abides in me and I in him, he it is that bears much fruit, for apart from me you can do nothing. John 15:5

Branches on a tree grow and produce fruit. Branches snapped off, or lying on the ground are gathered up and thrown away or burned. Every Christian is a branch. Jesus says so in John chapter 15. Branches do not create themselves! Each branch has its origin in the vine or tree. So also with members of God's family. We are not self-made Christians by our own doing or decision. Branches do not make the tree! Nor do branches choose a tree, or decide to be part of a tree. The vine or tree produces the branches. Life flows then, not from the branches to the tree, but from the tree to the branches! The order is important!

A Christian becomes a branch grafted into Christ the true Vine in Holy Baptism or through the preached message of Christ crucified and risen. You did not adopt Jesus; He adopted you as His child. Christ gave you life. You did not choose Jesus; He chose you and appointed you that you should bear much fruit (John 15:16).

After all, that is the purpose for the branch/vine--to bear fruit. If you own fruit trees such as an apple or orange tree, you look for fruit hanging on its branches. That's what God looks for in His people. Jesus doesn't wonder if He will find the fruits of faith in our lives; He *expects* to see them! God knows they will be there because that's what branches do who are growing in Christ--we bear fruit–fruit that will last!

In His great love for you, Jesus attached Himself to the tree of the cross to pay the ransom price for your sins. Jesus was willing to die in your place so that He could be the Source of life for you!

Christ died and rose again, and the life He lives is as much for you as it is for Him.

The devil, the sinful world, and our sinful flesh will try to convince you that your sins have severed you from Christ; that you are a worthless twig lying on the ground, fit only to be thrown into the fire, and that there is no hope for you. Do not listen to those lies!

Jesus' word of forgiveness is for everyone! It's the word of grace in your ears! It's the Word become flesh in bread and wine for you! This is how you "abide (remain) in Christ": through His Word--His word of forgiveness and peace! You are not a worthless stick! Your destiny is not to be pitched into the fire! By faith in Jesus, you are a precious branch that bears fruit because you are in Christ, and He is in you!

Rev. Philip Bloch

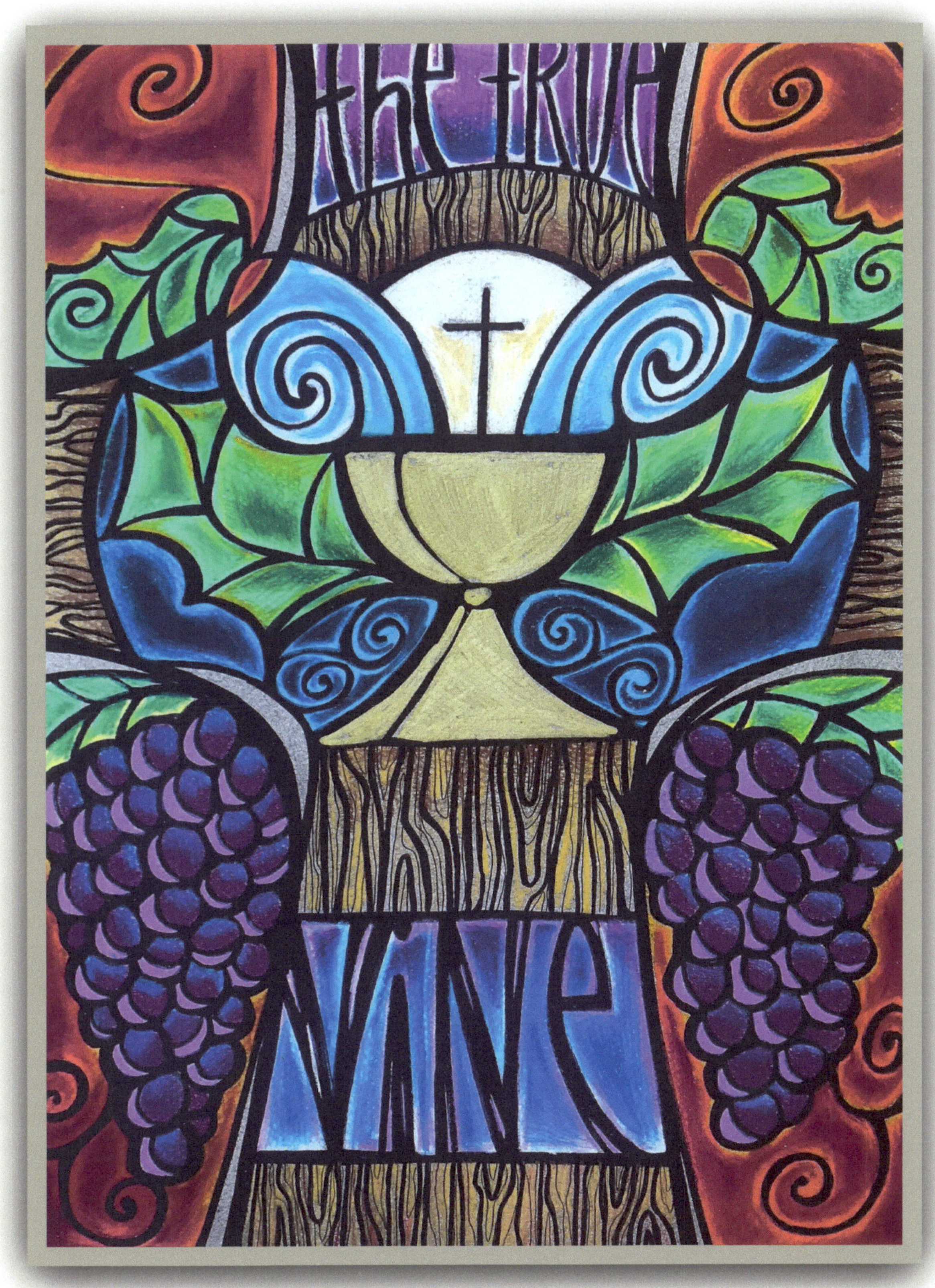

"The Vine and The Branches" - Ink and Watercolor

Sixth Sunday of Easter

Acts 10:34-48, 1 John 5:1-8, John 15:9-17

[Jesus said], These things I have spoken to you, that My joy may be in you, and that your joy may be full. John 15:11

The shortest verse in the English translation of the Bible is John 11:35 – "Jesus wept." The shortest verse in the Greek translation is 1 Thessalonians 5:16 – "...rejoice evermore." And if the entire Bible were taken away from us, leaving us only those two verses, we would have much hope because "Jesus wept" so we could "rejoice forevermore."

Now, that sounds like a dichotomy – weeping and rejoicing. But in Jesus we have reason to be joyful. Many times in the Bible Christians are reminded to be joyful. The Reformer, Martin Luther said this: "God is not a God of sadness and death, but the devil is. Christ is a God of joy, and so the Scriptures often say that we should rejoice...A Christian should and must be a cheerful person."

So, a Christian is called to be a joyful person. But nowhere in the Bible does it say that a Christian's life will be totally blissful and free from trials. The history of the Church bears this out. Many people would not renege on their belief in Jesus, choosing rather to die than turn their back on Him. It's because they had a joy knowing that heaven awaited them.

We too, when we struggle with relationship issues, with financial woes, with vocational setbacks, with health afflictions, with gut-wrenching grief can still find joy in Jesus. That joy comes in knowing and trusting that in the midst of all our problems is a God who knows our struggles because He lived as one of us on the earth. He knew sorrow; He knew pain; He know what it was liked to be abandoned by His friends and even His Father. Jesus suffered and wept on the cross on Calvary so our sins would be paid. And three days later, walking out of a grave very much alive, His power over death is now ours, and we look ahead to the glories of heaven and the Day Jesus will return.

Yes, joy in Jesus will stand when harsh words have brought us to our knees. Joy in Jesus can enable us to laugh again when grief has kicked us in the gut. Joy in Jesus can transform our **confusion** into **praise** and bring those who are down to be lifted up. My prayer is that you understand that joy and will cling to it all your lives.

Rev. James Rodriguez, Jr

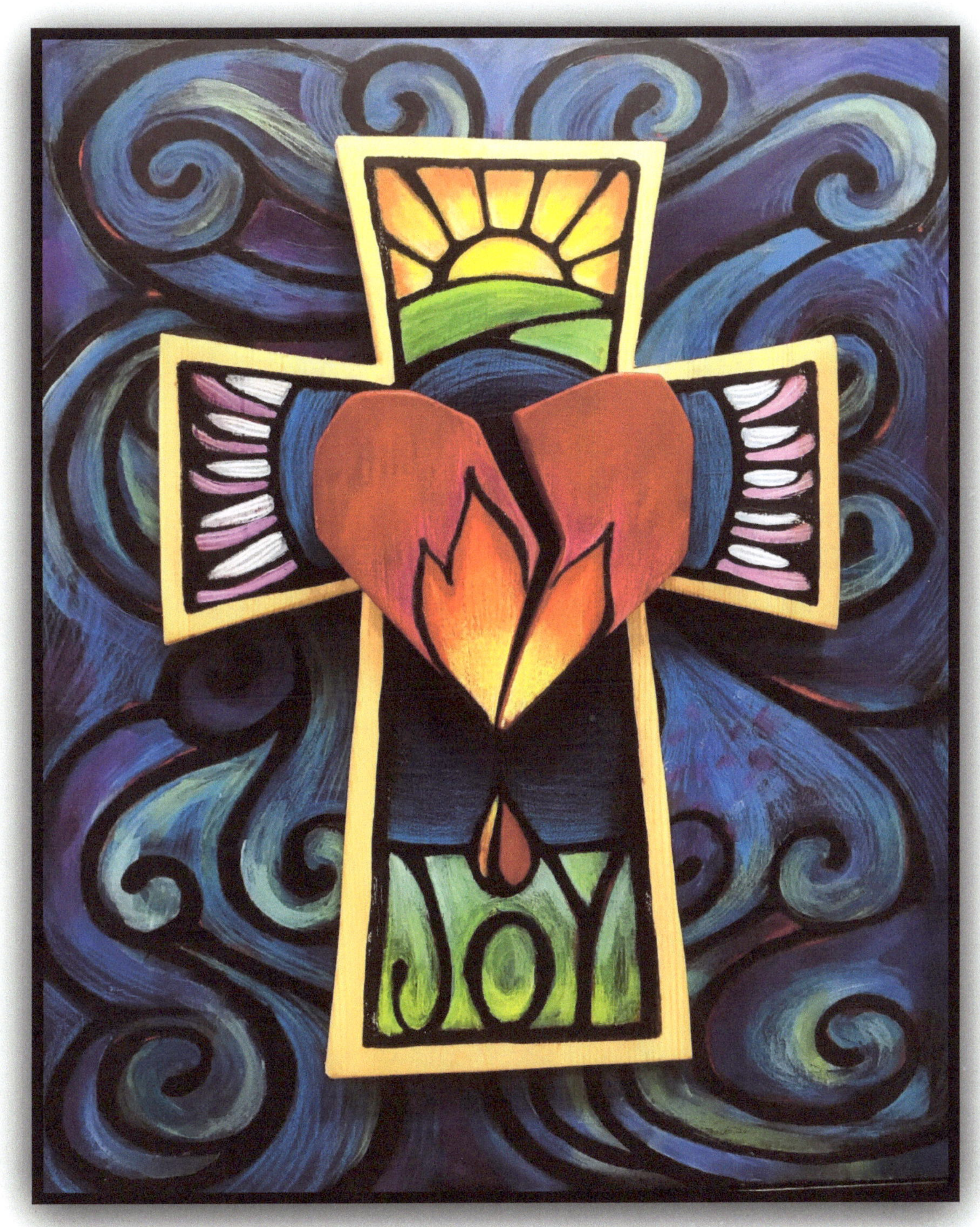

"Joy in Jesus" - Ink and Watercolor

The Ascension of Our Lord

Acts 1:1-11, Ephesians 1:15-23, Luke 24:44-53

See, the Lord Ascends in Triumph

See, the Lord ascends in triumph: Conqu'ring King in royal state,
Riding on the clouds, His chariot, To His heav'nly palace gate.
Hark! The choirs of angel voices Joyful alleluias sing,
And the portals high are lifted To receive their heav'nly King.

Who is this that comes in glory With the trump of jubilee?
Lord of battles, God of armies, He has gained the victory.
He who on the cross did suffer, He who from the grave arose.
He has vanquished sin and Satan; He by death has crushed His foes.

While He lifts His hands in blessing, He is parted from His friends;
While their eager eyes behold Him, He upon the clouds ascends.
He who walked with God and pleased Him, Preaching truth and doom to come,
He, our Enoch, is translated To His everlasting home.

Now our heav'nly Aaron enters With His blood within the veil;
Joshua now is come to Canaan, And the kings before Him quail.
Now He plants the tribes of Israel In their promised resting place:
Now our great Elijah offers Double portion of His grace.

He has raised our human nature On the clouds to God's right hand;
There we sit in heav'nly places, There with Him in glory stand.
Jesus reigns, adored by angels; Man with God is on the throne.
By our mighty Lord's ascension We by faith behold our own.

Christopher Wordsworth, 1807-1885

LSB 494

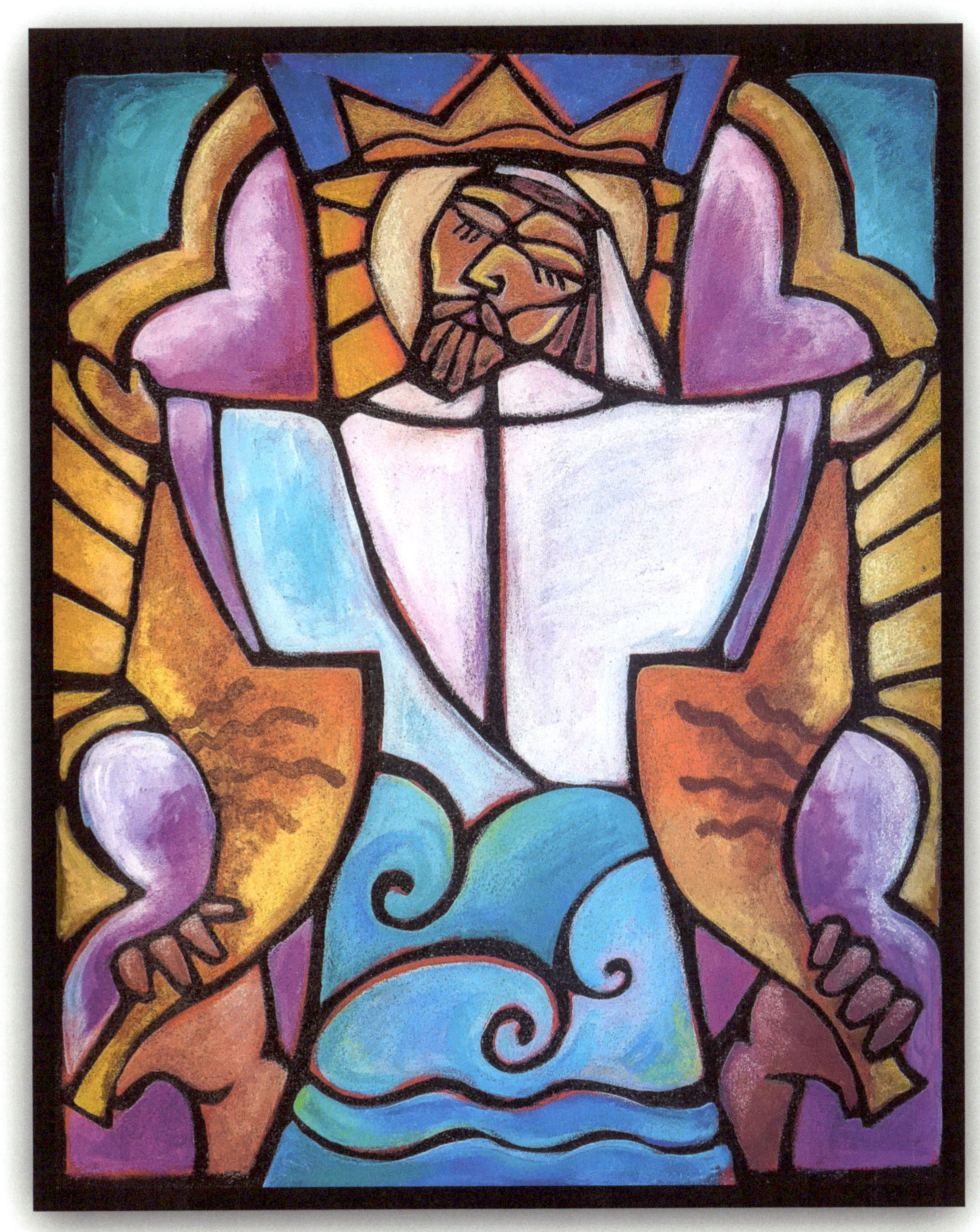

"Victorious Jubilee" - Acrylic on Wood

Seventh Sunday of Easter

Acts 1:12-26, 1 John 5:9-15, John 17:11b-19

All these with one accord were devoting themselves to prayer, together with the women and Mary the mother of Jesus and his brothers. Acts 1:14

In a Pew Research study, 76% of Americans reported that they pray daily or weekly. Nearly everyone prays sometimes. To be devoted to prayer is different. It means you treat it like your life depends on it.

Our reading from Acts is set in the Upper Room 40 days after Jesus rose from death. While nearly all of those in the Upper Room learned to pray as children, their devotion to prayer changed because of Jesus.

Jesus showed them what devotion is. Did He give up on them when they misunderstood what He said? No. Did He give up on them to save Himself? No.

Did Jesus quit on them when they scattered as He was arrested? No. Instead, He searched out and found them hiding in the upper room and showed them the scars of nails and spear. Jesus was devoted, committed to the mission of saving them and us from the power of sin and the destiny of death.

We live long after Jesus ascended. But He is still attentive to our voices. He promises to hear and answer us as we pray. Prayer sometimes gets a bad rap. After a terrorist attack in Paris, there was a hashtag, #prayforParis. There was another after Parkland. People genuinely prayed, but in both cases, critics said, "We don't need your prayers. We need action."

As if prayer and action are not related! Jesus was devoted to prayer, but it was never an excuse for Him not to **do**. To be devoted to prayer does not mean your hands can't work because they are always folded. Can you pray for your children, but never do anything for them?

Devotion to prayer is like filling the tank at the gas station, or charging the battery for your phone–it is preparation, not the goal. To be devoted to prayer is to believe that God hears and answers and acts.

Jesus is still devoted to you. He is loyal. He is faithful. He is dedicated. He forgives what is past. He invites you to start anew today. *We pray: Lord Jesus, help me faithfully speak to You in prayer and hear Your Word of promise to me. Amen*

Rev. Dr. Ralph Blomenberg

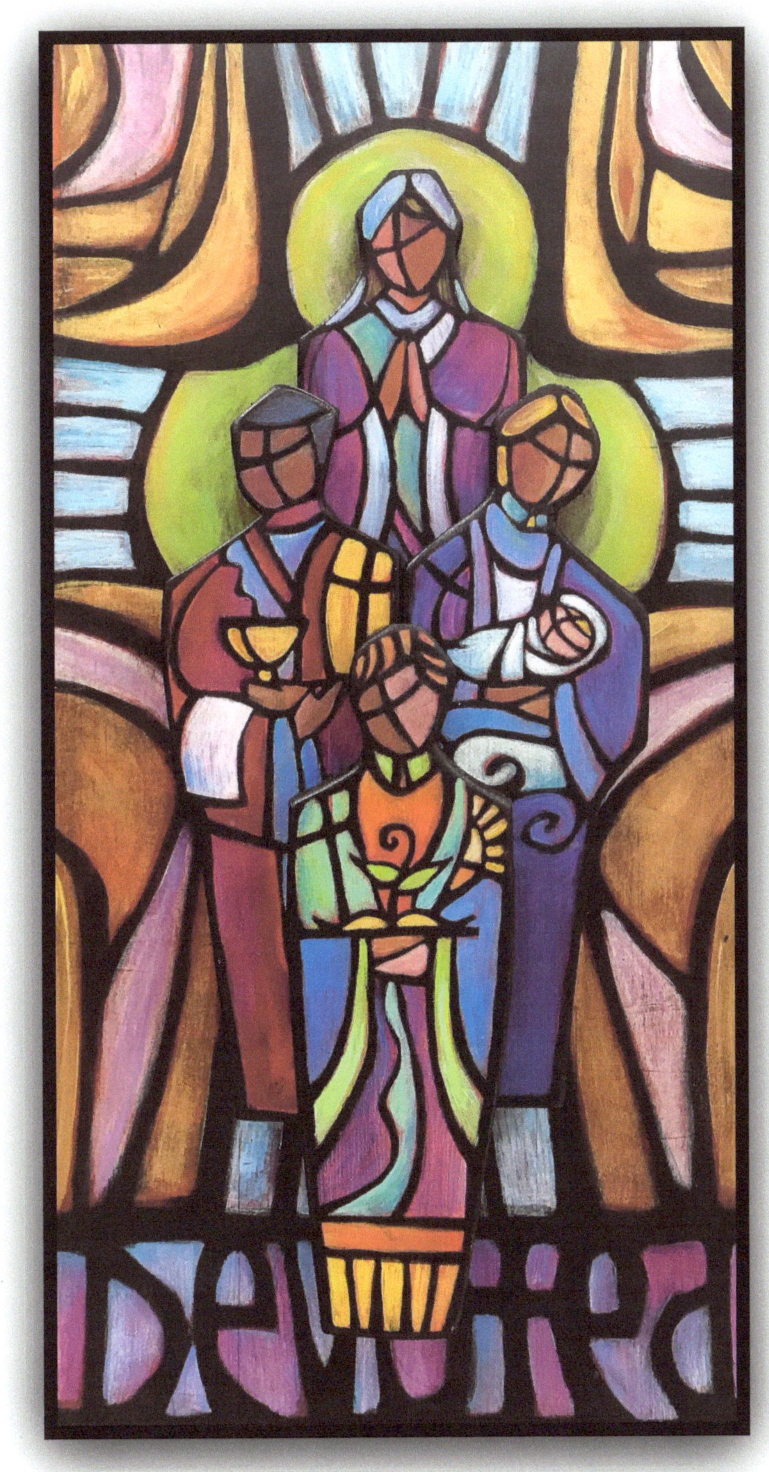

"Devoted" - Acrylic on Wood

www.ingramcontent.com/pod-product-compliance
Lightning Source LLC
LaVergne TN
LVHW070202110826
845147LV00002B/477

* 9 7 8 0 9 9 9 4 5 1 8 3 0 *